The Vision Board Book

Unleash Your Dreams, Empower Your Goals, and Manifest Your Future with Purpose and Creativity

In this Book you will find 500+ Elements from a Variety of Topics

- Wellness, Self-Care, Religion, Spirituality
- Learning, Knowledge, Study, Achievement
- Travel, Adventure, Exploration, Dedication
- Indulgence, Marriage, Friendship, Companionship
- Health, Food, Dining, Workout, Fitness
- Nature, Fauna, Flora, Mindfulness
- Home, Architecture, Dream Possessions
- Career, Work, Business, Finance
- Party and Celebration

Welcome to the exciting world of vision boards!

This clip art book with 500+ images, illustrations, quotes and affirmations is designed to help you create an inspiring and visually compelling vision board that brings your dreams and goals to life.

Why Vision Boards?

Vision boards are powerful tools that can help us manifest our desires and aspirations. By collecting and arranging images and words that represent our dreams, we create a visual representation of our goals, making them more tangible and achievable. They serve as a constant reminder of what we truly want, helping us stay motivated and focused on our journey toward success.

Who are Vision Boards useful for?

Vision boards are useful and sometimes necessary because **they stimulate our subconscious mind**, which in turn helps us make decisions and take actions aligned with our goals. They help us visualize the future we want to create, serving as an essential tool for personal growth and development. The process of curating images and words for your vision board also encourages self-reflection and introspection, which allows you to gain a deeper understanding of your values, passions, and priorities.

Vision boards are beneficial for people from all walks of life. They are especially helpful for individuals who need a boost of motivation, those facing major life changes, or anyone seeking clarity on their long-term goals. Whether you're an entrepreneur looking to grow your business, a student setting educational goals, or simply someone looking to **improve your overall well-being**, a vision board can be a transformative and inspiring tool.

With this vision board clip art book, you'll have access to a wide variety of images and phrases that can be used to create a personalized vision board. The journey toward your dreams starts now - let your imagination run wild and enjoy the process of designing a vision board that reflects your unique aspirations and ambitions.

Create Your Personalized Vision Board
A Fun and Transformative Experience

Here are a few **tips to help you create an effective and inspiring vision board**:

- **Set clear intentions**: Before you begin, take some time to reflect on your goals and aspirations. Consider what you want to achieve in various areas of your life, such as relationships, career, health, and personal growth.
- **Gather materials**: Use the images and quotes from this clip art book that resonate with you to make your vision board visually appealing.
- **Choose a base**: Decide on the type of board you want to use, such as a corkboard, foam board, or poster board. Ensure that the board is large enough to accommodate your chosen images and quotes.
- **Organize and arrange**: Start by sorting through your collected materials and selecting the images and words that best represent your goals. Experiment with different layouts, placing the most important elements in the center of the board and working outward.
- **Be creative**: Don't be afraid to get creative with your vision board. Use scissors to cut out unique shapes, or layer images and text to add depth and interest. You can also use colored markers, paint, or washi tape to add a personal touch.
- **Stay focused**: Keep your vision board simple and focused. Too many images or words can be overwhelming and dilute the impact of your message. Aim for clarity and coherence to make your board more effective.
- **Display your vision board**: Once completed, place your vision board in a prominent location where you can see it daily. This will serve as a constant reminder of your goals and help keep you motivated.
- **Update regularly**: As your goals and priorities evolve, update your vision board to reflect these changes. This will help you stay aligned with your current aspirations and maintain your motivation.
- **Visualize and take action**: Use your vision board as a tool for visualization. Spend time each day imagining yourself achieving your goals, and then take small steps toward making those dreams a reality.
- **Share your vision**: If you feel comfortable, share your vision board with friends or family members. This can provide additional motivation and support, as well as hold you accountable to your goals.

Remember that **creating a vision board is a personal journey**, and there's no right or wrong way to do it. Trust your intuition and enjoy the process of designing a board that reflects your unique aspirations and desires.

How to Pick the Best Ingredients

Here are some **tips for** choosing meaningful images, words, and symbols:

- **Focus on emotions**: Choose images, words, and symbols that evoke strong positive emotions in you. This will help create a deeper connection with your goals and motivate you to take action.

- **Be specific**: Opt for visuals that represent your goals as specifically as possible. For example, if your goal is to travel to Paris, include an image of the Eiffel Tower rather than a generic picture of an airplane.

- **Quality matters**: We have select high-quality images with clear colors and details for you to add to your vision board. This will make your vision board more visually appealing and help you focus on your goals.

- **Personal relevance**: Choose words, quotes, and symbols that have personal significance to you. This might include a favorite quote from a book, an inspiring phrase from a mentor, or a symbol that represents a core value.

- **Mix and match**: Combine different types of visuals, such as photographs, illustrations, and typography. This adds variety and texture to your vision board, making it more engaging and inspiring.

- **Consider color psychology**: Use colors that evoke the feelings and energy you want to bring into your life. For example, blue or aqua can represent calm and stability, while red or purple can symbolize passion and action.

- **Align with your values**: Select images, words, and symbols that align with your core values and beliefs. This will help you stay true to yourself and maintain focus on what truly matters to you.

- **Use positive language**: Choose words and phrases that convey optimism, encouragement, and self-belief. This will help reinforce a positive mindset and motivate you to take action toward your goals.

- **Don't overthink it**: Trust your intuition when selecting visuals for your vision board. If an image or phrase resonates with you on an emotional level, it's likely a good fit for your board.

- **Keep it balanced**: While it's essential to have ambitious goals, include images and words that represent self-care, relaxation, and personal growth. This will help ensure your vision board is balanced and promotes a healthy, holistic approach to achieving your dreams.

- **Layer and experiment**: Don't be afraid to layer images, words, and symbols to create depth and visual interest. This can also help you explore the connections between your goals and identify potential synergies that could accelerate your progress.

- **Leave room for growth**: Consider leaving some empty space on your vision board to allow for new goals, dreams, and ideas to emerge as you grow and evolve. This will help keep your vision board flexible and adaptive to change.

Techniques to Overcome Mental Roadblocks and Maintain Focus

- **Break goals into smaller tasks**: Large goals can feel overwhelming, making it difficult to maintain focus. Break them down into smaller, achievable tasks to make progress more manageable and maintain motivation.
- **Visualization**: Regularly visualize yourself achieving your goals and experiencing the positive emotions associated with success. This will help reinforce your commitment and keep you focused on your objectives.
- **Positive affirmations**: Use positive affirmations to counteract negative thoughts and self-doubt. Repeat affirmations <u>daily</u> to rewire your brain for success and maintain a positive mindset.
- **Surround yourself with support**: Build a network of supportive people who encourage your goals and dreams. Share your vision board with them, and lean on them for encouragement, guidance, and accountability.
- **Set deadlines**: Establish deadlines for your goals to create a sense of urgency and maintain focus. Regularly review and adjust your deadlines as needed to stay on track.
- **Practice mindfulness**: Engage in mindfulness practices like meditation, deep breathing, or yoga to help manage stress, maintain focus, and enhance mental clarity.
- **Journaling**: Write down your thoughts, feelings, and progress in a journal. This will help you track your growth, identify mental roadblocks, and develop strategies to overcome them.
- **Embrace setbacks**: Recognize that setbacks are a natural part of personal growth. Learn from them, adapt your approach, and use the experience to strengthen your resolve.
- **Reward yourself**: Celebrate your achievements, no matter how small. Acknowledging your progress will help maintain motivation and reinforce your commitment to your goals.
- **Time management techniques**: Use time management techniques like the Pomodoro Technique or time blocking to improve productivity and maintain focus on your goals. Dedicate specific time periods to working on your tasks and minimize distractions during these periods.
- **Gratitude practice**: Cultivate a gratitude practice by regularly reflecting on the things you're grateful for in your life. This will help you maintain a positive mindset, shift your focus away from obstacles, and stay motivated to pursue your goals.
- **Review and revise**: Regularly review your vision board and the progress you've made toward your goals. Adjust your approach as needed to overcome mental roadblocks and maintain focus on your objectives.

The Law of Attraction

The Law of Attraction is a philosophical concept that suggests we can attract into our lives whatever we are focusing on. It is rooted in the idea that all thoughts eventually turn into things. Therefore, if you focus on negative doom and gloom, you will remain under that cloud, but if you focus on positive thoughts and have goals that you aim to achieve, you will find a way to achieve them with action.

This belief is based on the idea that individuals and their thoughts are made from pure energy, and through the process of manifestation, visualization and action a person can improve their own health, wealth, and personal relationships. The Law of Attraction is not universally accepted, and its effectiveness is believed to be a combination of intrinsic belief, focused intention, and pattern-seeking behavior.

It is thought that The Law of Attraction operates on a few key principles:

- **Like Attracts Like**: This principle proposes that similar thoughts, emotions, or mental states tend to cluster together, influencing the individual's perception of reality and their experiences. Therefore, positive thoughts will attract positive outcomes, while negative thoughts will lead to undesired results.
- **Nature Abhors a Vacuum**: This suggests that removing negative things from your life can make room for more positive things to take their place.
- **The Present is Always Perfect**: This principle focuses on the idea of living in the present and appreciating what you have now, which serves as a foundation for attracting future abundance.
- **The Law of Action**: While not traditionally included, this principle is often associated with the Law of Attraction to denote that it's not enough to simply think and feel - one must also take action to manifest what one desires.

Vision boards serve as a tangible and powerful manifestation tool for the Law of Attraction, providing a **constant visual reminder** of your dreams, goals, and aspirations. By selecting images and words that align with your desired outcomes and arranging them on your vision board, you're actively focusing your thoughts on what you want to attract in your life. This **consistent visual cue stimulates** the emotional and cognitive states that align with your desires, helping to keep your attention on your intentions. As you regularly view and engage with your vision board, you're affirming your aspirations, and according to the Law of Attraction, drawing those very experiences and resources into your reality. Therefore, **vision boards are a practical application of the Law of Attraction, turning your positive thoughts and desires into a visual, interactive, and dynamic reality**.

Wish List

Date Fom _____ To _____

- [ ] _____
- [ ] _____
- [ ] _____
- [ ] _____
- [ ] _____
- [ ] _____
- [ ] _____
- [ ] _____
- [ ] _____
- [ ] _____
- [ ] _____
- [ ] _____
- [ ] _____
- [ ] _____
- [ ] _____

- [ ] _____
- [ ] _____
- [ ] _____
- [ ] _____
- [ ] _____
- [ ] _____
- [ ] _____
- [ ] _____
- [ ] _____
- [ ] _____
- [ ] _____
- [ ] _____
- [ ] _____
- [ ] _____
- [ ] _____

Purpose: A wish list is a collection of desired items or experiences that you would like to have, often in a shorter time frame. Wish lists can be more casual and less focused on personal growth or fulfillment.
Scope: Wish lists are short-term or ongoing, with items that can be easily added or removed as a person's desires or circumstances change. They may include more immediate or easily attainable items.
Items: Items on a wish list tend to be material possessions, experiences, or smaller-scale personal goals. Examples include new electronic gadgets, attending a specific concert, or trying out a new hobby.

Bucket List

Date Fom _____ To _____

- [ ] _____
- [ ] _____
- [ ] _____
- [ ] _____
- [ ] _____
- [ ] _____
- [ ] _____
- [ ] _____
- [ ] _____
- [ ] _____
- [ ] _____
- [ ] _____
- [ ] _____
- [ ] _____

- [ ] _____
- [ ] _____
- [ ] _____
- [ ] _____
- [ ] _____
- [ ] _____
- [ ] _____
- [ ] _____
- [ ] _____
- [ ] _____
- [ ] _____
- [ ] _____
- [ ] _____
- [ ] _____

Purpose: A bucket list consists of experiences or accomplishments a person wants to achieve within their lifetime. It is a compilation of significant goals or milestones that hold personal meaning and contribute to a sense of fulfillment.

Scope: Bucket lists are typically long-term and contain a mix of realistic and ambitious goals. These goals often require planning, effort, and resources to achieve.

Items: Items on a bucket list are diverse and can include travel destinations, career milestones, personal growth experiences, or adventure activities. Examples might be visiting the Great Wall of China, running a marathon, or learning a new language.

I matter

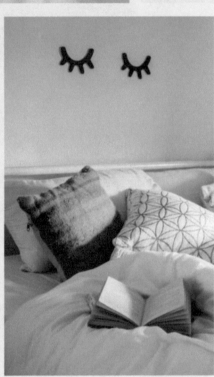

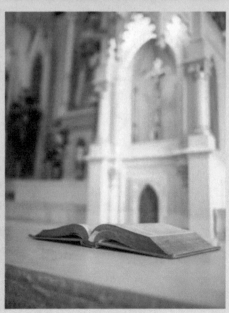

meditation

exist to
be happy
not to
impress...

girl power

**DON'T LET YOUR
MIND BULLY
YOUR BODY**

ERFECT

TY

BO

HEALTH

The longer I stay at home,
the more homeless I look.

SILENCE
IS BETTER
THAN
BULLSHIT!

LET LIFE
SURPRISE
YOU

TRAVEL IS GOOD FOR THE SOUL

VAC♥Y mode

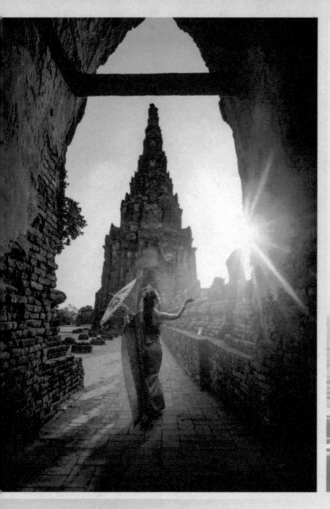

do what
you love

BREATHE

PROTECT THE OCEANS

COME OVER AND JOIN US

VOLUNTEER

FRAGILE

FRAGILE

FOOD

FOOD

Medicine

Let the
real you shine

HAVE
a
DREAM

Tuba City 11
Kayenta 82

3KAR503

Aloha Summer

LVE

THIS IS WHAT BEING IN LOVE REALLY MEANS, BECAUSE IT'S NOT ALL SEX AND KISSES

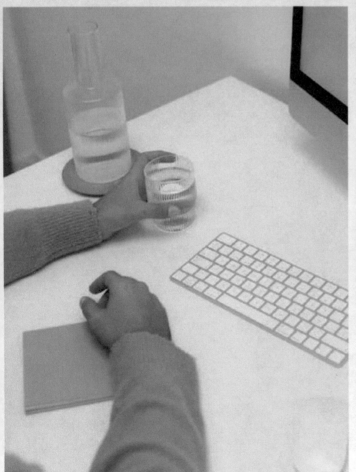

8 AM- READY. SET. DRINK!

10 AM- YOU'VE GOT IT

12 PM- KEEP DRINKING

2 PM- HALFWAY THERE!

4 PM- NO EXCUSES

6 PM- A LITTLE BIT MORE

8 PM- YOU MADE IT!

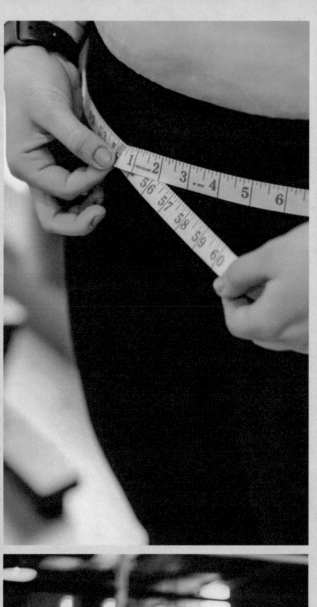

WAKE UP & WORKOUT

I'M DOING
THIS FOR ME

NO TIME
FOR
FAKE PEOPLE

WORRY
LESS
LIVE
MORE

impossible

NEW
HOME

TIME
FOR
CHANGE

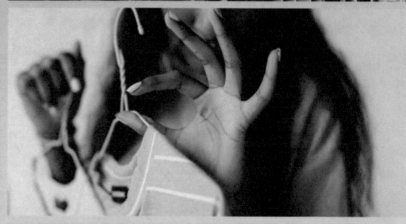

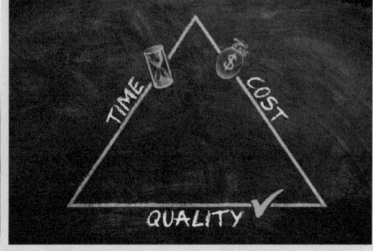

FINANCIAL
FREEDOM

no risk no story

Be Brilliant

DOUBT

WORK FROM HOME

THINK ABOUT THINGS DIFFERENTLY

I HATE NOTHING ABOUT U

look
at
you

I
CAN
THEREFORE
I
AM

BELIEVE YOU CAN AND YOU'RE HALFWAY THERE."
- THEODORE ROOSEVELT

"The question isn't who is going to let me; it's who is going to stop me."
- Ayn Rand

"Success is not final, failure is not fatal: It is the courage to continue that counts."
– Winston Churchill

"Do not wait for leaders; do it alone, person to person."
- Mother Teresa

"The only way to do great work is to love what you do."
- Steve Jobs

"The most effective way to do it is to do it."
- Amelia Earhart

"The best time to plant a tree was 20 years ago. The second best time is now."
- Chinese Proverb

"Your life does not get better by chance, it gets better by change."
- Jim Rohn

"No one can make you feel inferior without your consent."
- Eleanor Roosevelt

"The only limit to our realization of tomorrow will be our doubts of today."
- Franklin D. Roosevelt

"The only way to achieve the impossible is to believe it is possible."
- Alice Walker

"IF YOU DON'T RISK ANYTHING, YOU RISK EVEN MORE."
– ERICA JONG

"Do not wait; the time will never be 'just right.' Start where you stand, and work with whatever tools you may have at your command, and better tools will be found as you go along."
- George Herbert

"You miss 100% of the shots you don't take."
— Wayne Gretzky

"What you do makes a difference, and you have to decide what kind of difference you want to make."
— Jane Goodall

"Don't watch the clock; do what it does. Keep going."
— Sam Levenson

"It's never too late to be what you might have been."
— George Eliot (Mary Anne Evans)

"Success is liking yourself, liking what you do, and liking how you do it."
— Maya Angelou

"Act as if what you do makes a difference. It does."
— William James

"In the middle of every difficulty lies opportunity."
— Albert Einstein

"YOU ARE NEVER TOO OLD TO SET ANOTHER GOAL OR TO DREAM A NEW DREAM."
— C.S. LEWIS

"Believe in yourself. You are braver than you think, more talented than you know, and capable of more than you imagine."
— Roy T. Bennett

"The harder you work for something, the greater you'll feel when you achieve it."
— Anonymous

"Everything you've ever wanted is on the other side of fear."
— George Addair

"What lies behind us and what lies before us are tiny matters compared to what lies within us."
– Ralph Waldo Emerson

"I CAN'T THINK OF ANY BETTER REPRESENTATION OF BEAUTY THAN SOMEONE WHO IS UNAFRAID TO BE HERSELF."
– EMMA STONE

"The secret of getting ahead is getting started."
– Mark Twain

"You can't be that kid standing at the top of the waterslide, overthinking it. You have to go down the chute."
– Tina Fey

"Don't be intimidated by what you don't know. That can be your greatest strength and ensure that you do things differently from everyone else."
– Sara Blakely

"I choose to make the rest of my life the best of my life."
– Louise Hay

"Don't be pushed around by the fears in your mind. Be led by the dreams in your heart."
– Roy T. Bennett

"YOU MUST DO THE THINGS YOU THINK YOU CANNOT DO."
– ELEANOR ROOSEVELT

"The only thing that will stop you from fulfilling your dreams is you."
– Tom Bradley

"You may not control all the events that happen to you, but you can decide not to be reduced by them."
– Maya Angelou

"THE MOST COMMON WAY PEOPLE GIVE UP THEIR POWER IS BY THINKING THEY DON'T HAVE ANY."
- ALICE WALKER

"Success is not the key to happiness. Happiness is the key to success. If you love what you are doing, you will be successful."
- Albert Schweitzer

"Doubt kills more dreams than failure ever will."
- Suzy Kassem

"When one door of happiness closes, another opens; but often we look so long at the closed door that we do not see the one which has been opened for us."
- Helen Keller

"The future belongs to those who believe in the beauty of their dreams."
- Eleanor Roosevelt

"I've learned that people will forget what you said, people will forget what you did, but people will never forget how you made them feel."
- Maya Angelou

"The most courageous act is still to think for yourself. Aloud."
- Coco Chanel

"You should never let your fears prevent you from doing what you know is right."
- Aung San Suu Kyi

"The biggest adventure you can take is to live the life of your dreams."
- Oprah Winfrey

Dream big, start small, act now!

TURN OBSTACLES INTO Opportunities

Take action, make progress

Embrace change, seek growth

Find balance, find happiness

Never give up, keep pushing forward

Chase your dreams not competition

TRANSFORM FEAR INTO FUEL

CONSISTENCY *breeds* SUCCESS

Live with PURPOSE, PASSION, and PERSISTENCE

Rise above challenges, soar to success

Doubt less, achieve more

LEARN, GROW, CONQUER

CREATE YOUR OWN DESTINY

PROGRESS over Perfection

FIND STRENGTH IN VULNERABILITY

Cultivate gratitude, cultivate joy

CELEBRATE SMALL WINS, EMBRACE BIG *dreams*

Trust the *journey*, trust *yourself*

EMBRACE FAILURE, IT'S PART OF SUCCESS

Stay curious,
Stay inspired

KEEP
MOVING,
KEEP
GROWING

I choose
growth
over
comfort

Inhale
courage,
exhale
fear

EMPOWER YOURSELF, EMPOWER OTHERS

You are your only limit

PATIENCE, PERSISTENCE, AND PERSEVERANCE

I TRUST MY JOURNEY AND MY INTUITION

I am UNSTOPPABLE

I embrace my inner strength

OWN YOUR STORY, OWN YOUR SUCCESS

FEAR IS TEMPORARY, REGRET IS FOREVER

Life begins at the edge of your COMFORT ZONE

Visualize, Believe, Achieve

Choose **Courage** *over* COMFORT

Let passion be your guide

STAY HUNGRY STAY HUMBLE

Unlock your Potential

BE PRESENT, BE MINDFUL, BE GRATEFUL

BELIEVE IN THE POWER OF CHANGE

ONE STEP AT A TIME

I am the ARCHITECT of my life

Stay focused, stay determined

BE BRAVE BE BOLD

I believe in

MYSELF

I am

LIMITLESS

I am

EVOLVING

I am

UNIQUE

I can

OVERCOME

I am

COURAGEOUS

I believe in

CHANGE

I achieve

GREATNESS

I am blessed with

TALENTS

I am driven by

PASSION

I embrace

DIVERSITY

I focus on

PROGRESS

I am mindful

of my

TIME

I am

CREATIVE

I manifest

ABUNDANCE

I pursue

HAPPINESS

I conquer

CHALLENGES

I attract

POSITIVITY

I cultivate

LOVE

I radiate

CONFIDENCE

Monday	January	July
Tuesday	February	August
Wednesday	March	September
Thursday	April	October
Friday	May	November
Saturday	June	December
Sunday		
	Morning	Spring
Day	Noon	Evening	Summer
Night	Afternoon	Fall	Winter

add	Success	Love
add	Goals	Creativity
add	Dream	Fitness
add	Inspire	Balance
add	Passion	Gratitude
add	Confidence	Mindfulness
more	Health	Adventure
more	Wealth	Growth
more	Happiness	Motivation
more	Travel	Peace
more	Family	Courage

Joy	Positivity
Empower	Self-love
Focus	Career
Abundance	Relaxation
Prosperity	Resilience
Freedom	Purpose
Knowledge	Friendship
Strength	Connection
Vision	Compassion
Wisdom	Ambition
Achievement	Wellness

Learning	Transformation
Spirituality	Intuition
Innovation	Perseverance
Discipline	Confidence
Determination	Adventure
Patience	Authenticity
Harmony	Mindset
Fulfillment	Collaboration
Exploration	Self-discovery
Expression	Generosity
Opportunity	Reflection

Renewal	Independence
Gratitude	Legacy
Serenity	Mastery
Resilience	Nourishment
Breakthrough	Optimism
Commitment	Persistence
Curiosity	Rejuvenation
Endurance	Self-care
Enthusiasm	Trust
Imagination	Vitality
Impact	Zeal

Achieve	Explore
Create	Pursue
Inspire	Dream
Manifest	Overcome
Grow	Connect
Succeed	Believe
Transform	Nurture
Empower	Focus
Discover	Evolve
Thrive	Embrace
Innovate	Collaborate

Quickly	Quietly
Gently	Eagerly
Easily	Never
Always	Suddenly
Rarely	Directly
Clearly	Gracefully
Slowly	Honestly
Frequently	Efficiently
Carefully	Cautiously
Happily	Patiently
Enthusiastically	Boldly

We hope that **"The Vision Board Book: Unleash Your Dream, Empower Your Goals, and Manifest Your Future with Purpose and Creativity"** has empowered you to tap into the power of visualization and manifest your deepest aspirations. If you've enjoyed the journey, crafted an inspiring vision board, and found the images, illustrations, affirmations, and quotes valuable, we'd absolutely love to hear about your experiences.

We would be immensely grateful if you could take a few moments to leave a review on **Amazon**. Your **feedback** is incredibly important to us, as it helps us continually refine our work and inspire others on their journey of personal transformation.

Please share your thoughts, successes, or any transformative moments and stories you've had while using "The Vision Board Book" at **inspiranexus@gmail.com**. Remember, your story could be the inspiration that empowers someone else to unleash their dreams. Thank you for being a part of our community, and we look forward to hearing about your journey towards manifesting your dream life.

NEVER EVER QUIT

InspiraNexus
PRESS

Made in United States
Troutdale, OR
12/29/2024